To order additional copies of this book, con-
tact:
Xlibris
0800-443-678
www.xlibris.co.nz
Orders@ Xlibris.co.nz

For all lovers of bugs

Out in my garden. Hiding all around. In the trees or in the leaves or crawling on the ground. You might see something creeping, something big or small. You might just find an insect friend so listen for their call...

Abdomen

Thorax

Head

Spur

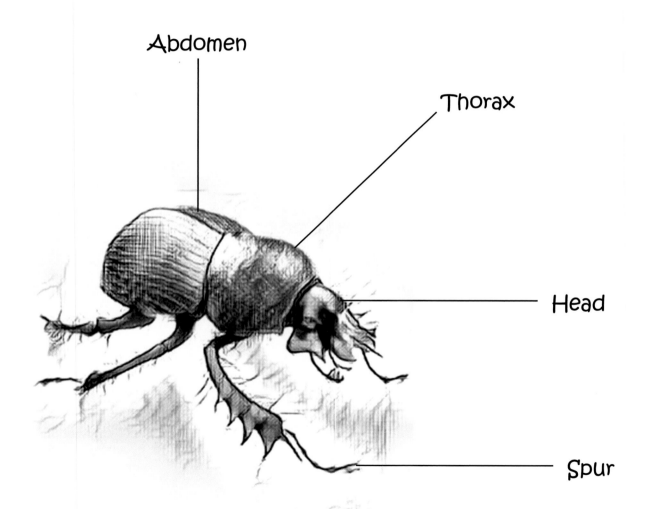

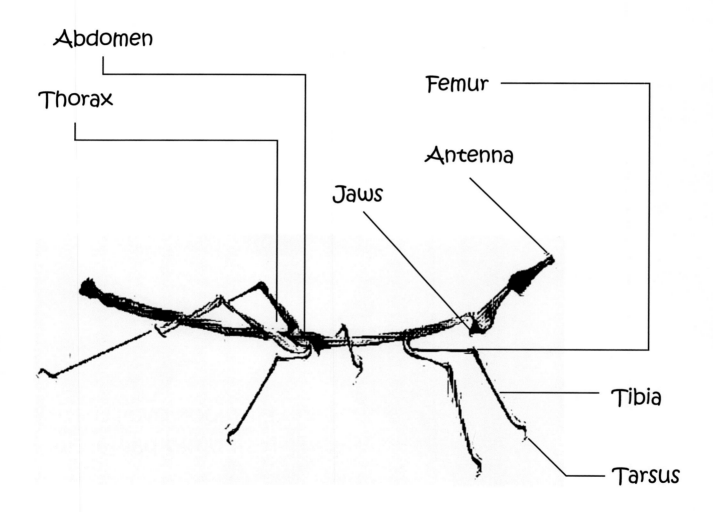

Abdomen

Thorax

Femur

Antenna

Jaws

Tibia

Tarsus

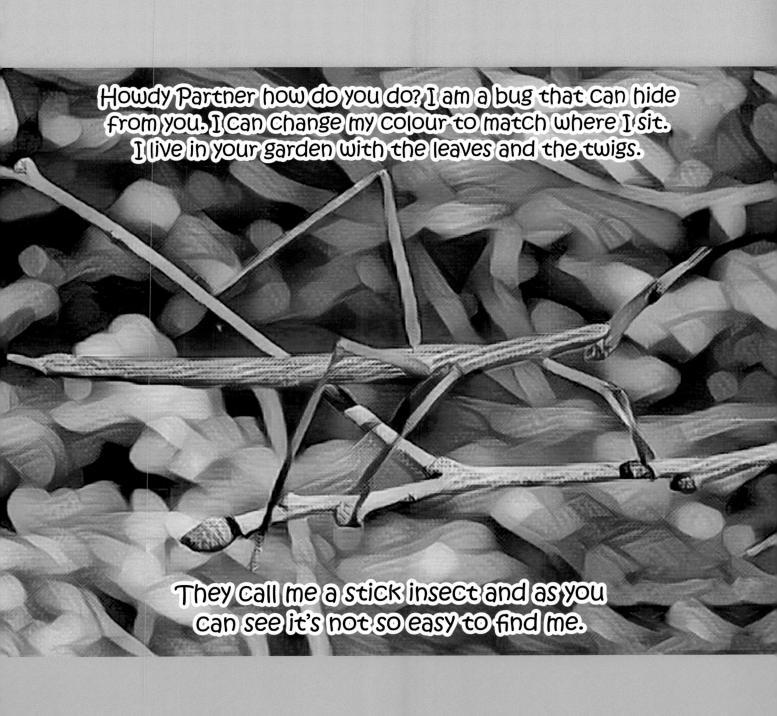

Howdy Partner how do you do? I am a bug that can hide from you. I can change my colour to match where I sit. I live in your garden with the leaves and the twigs.

They call me a stick insect and as you can see it's not so easy to find me.

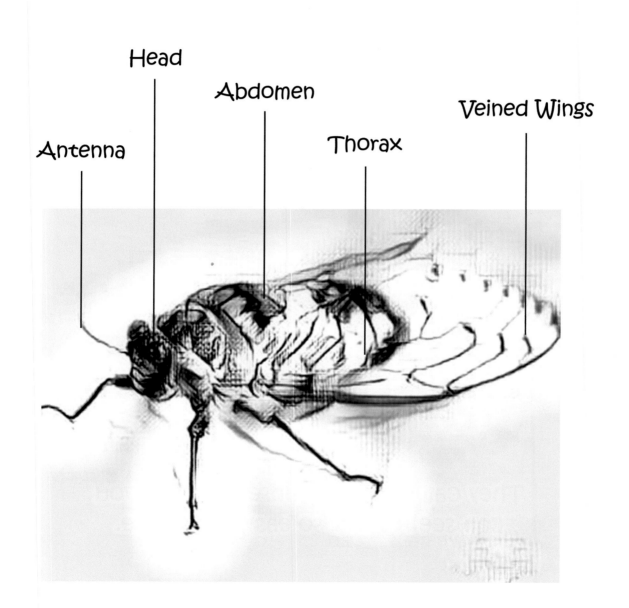

Sometimes at night or late in the day,
You can hear me calling from far away.
You might find my shell stuck to a tree.
Then I spread my new wings and fly free.

Cicada is my name can you hear my song?

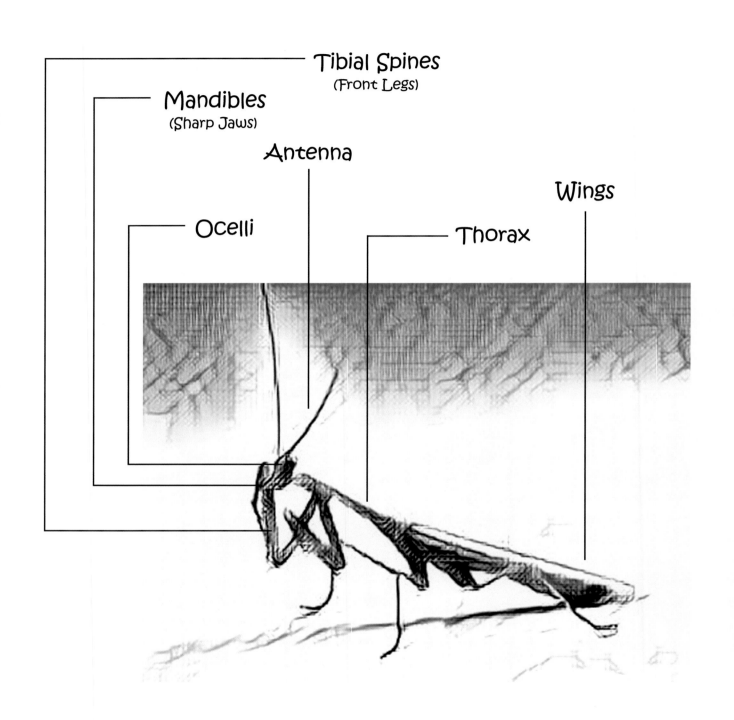

Tibial Spines
(Front Legs)

Mandibles
(Sharp Jaws)

Antenna

Ocelli

Wings

Thorax

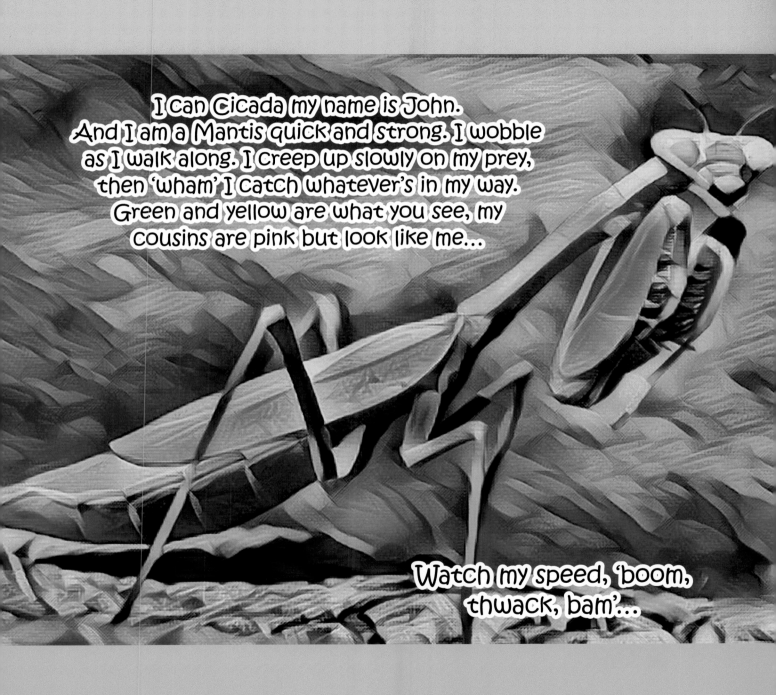

Antenna

Scutellum

Elytron

Pronotum

Tarsus

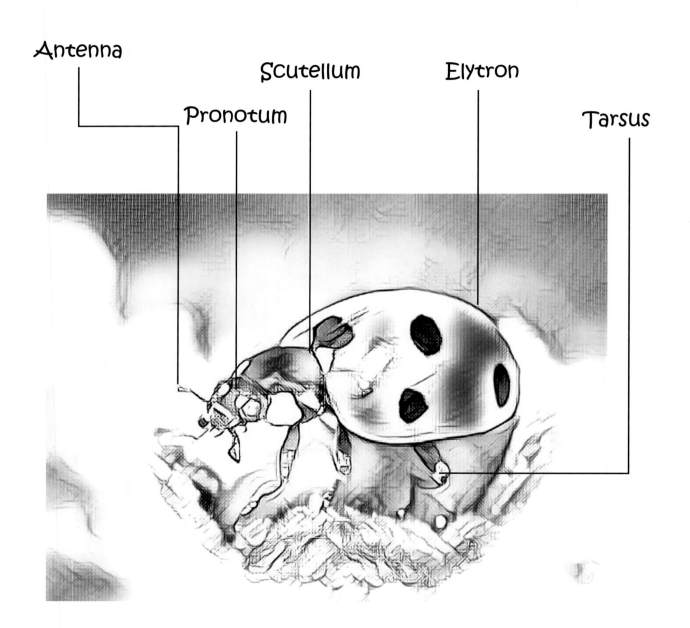

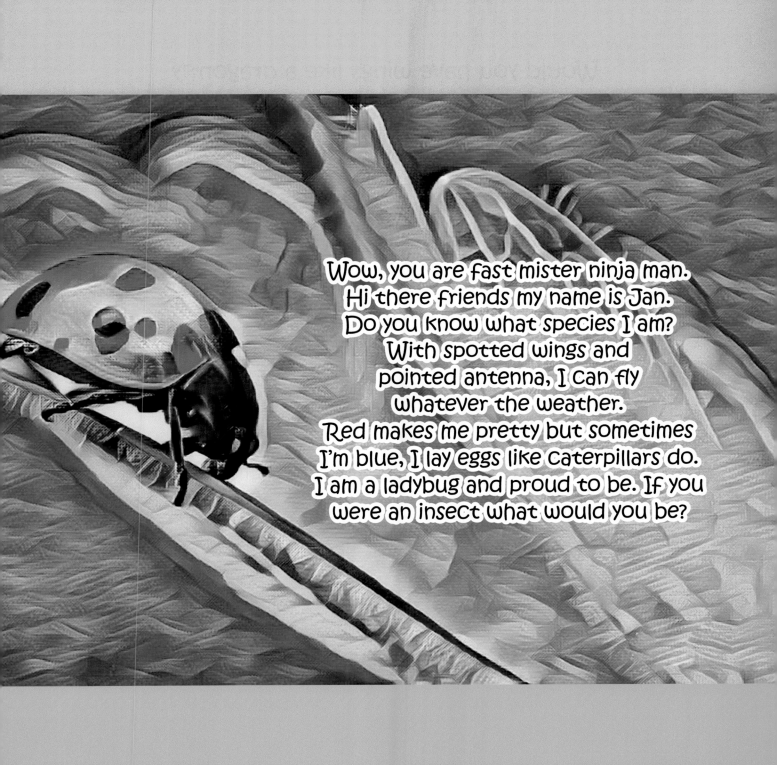

Wow, you are fast mister ninja man.
Hi there friends my name is Jan.
Do you know what species I am?
With spotted wings and
pointed antenna, I can fly
whatever the weather.
Red makes me pretty but sometimes
I'm blue, I lay eggs like caterpillars do.
I am a ladybug and proud to be. If you
were an insect what would you be?

Would you have wings like a dragonfly
The fastest insect in the sky.

6 Jointed Legs

2 Pair of
Transparent Wings

Segmented
Abdominal

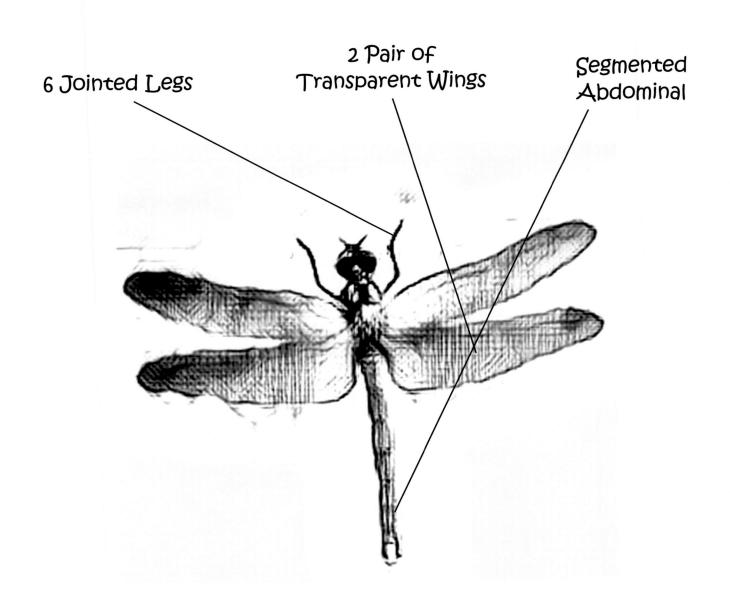

Perhaps you would wiggle like a worm or a slug.
Or have a secret weapon like a little stink bug.

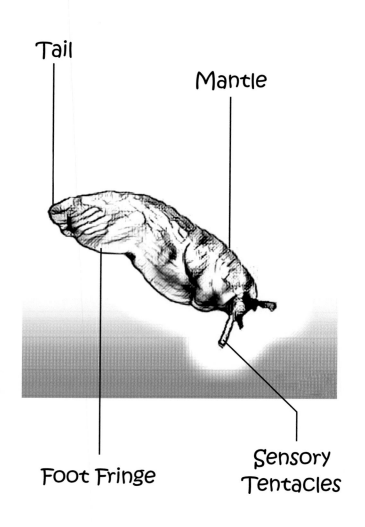

Tail

Mantle

Foot Fringe

Sensory
Tentacles

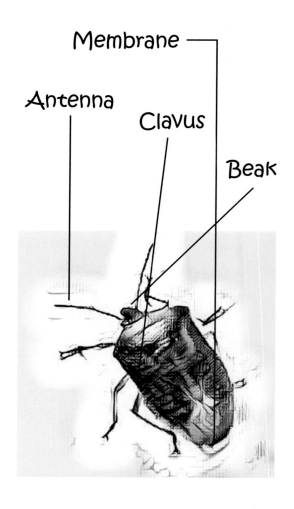

Membrane

Antenna

Clavus

Beak

Out in the garden. Crawling all around,
Are fascinating creatures just waiting to be found.

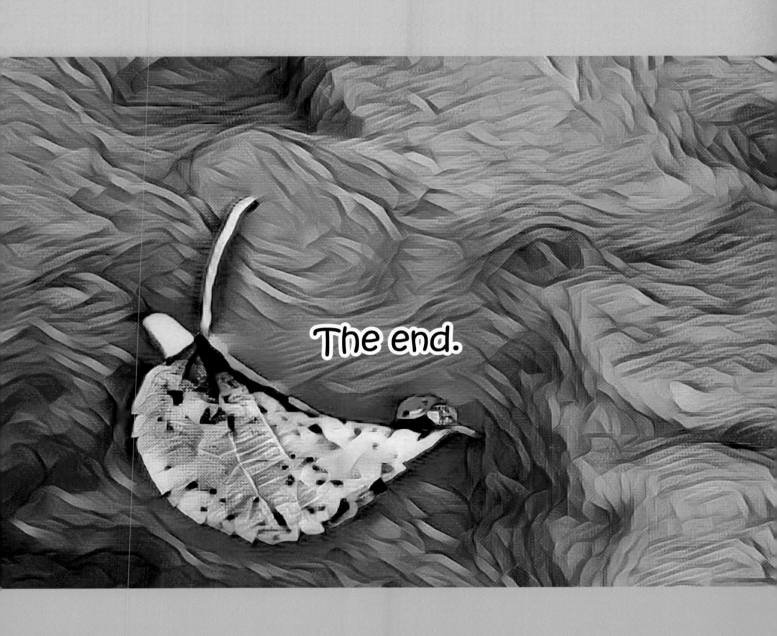

The end.

Printed in the United States
By Bookmasters